THE CHRISTMAS STORY

Illustrated by Elisa Trimby

FABER AND FABER
London   Boston

Illustrations copyright © 1983 by Elisa Trimby
Extracts from the Authorized King James Version of the Bible,
which is Crown Copyright, are reproduced by permission.
First published in Great Britain in 1983 by Faber and Faber Limited.
All rights reserved. No part of this book may be reproduced or
utilized in any form or by any means, electronic or mechanical,
including photocopying, recording, or by any information storage and
retrieval system, without permission in writing from the Publisher.
Inquiries should be addressed to Lothrop, Lee & Shepard Books, a
division of William Morrow & Company, Inc., 105 Madison Avenue,
New York, New York 10016.

Printed in Great Britain. First U.S. Edition. 1 2 3 4 5 6 7 8 9 10
CIP available
ISBN 0-688-02444-0
ISBN 0-688-02458-0 (lib. bdg.)

84 923

LOTHROP, LEE & SHEPARD BOOKS
NEW YORK

9003

IN THE days of Herod the King, the angel Gabriel was sent from God unto a city of Galilee, named Nazareth,

To a virgin espoused to a man whose name was Joseph, of the house of David; and the virgin's name was Mary.

And the angel came in unto her, and said, Hail, thou that art highly favoured, the Lord is with thee: blessed art thou among women.

And when she saw him, she was troubled at his saying, and cast in her mind what manner of salutation this should be.

And the angel said unto her, Fear not, Mary: for thou hast found favour with God.

And, behold, thou shalt conceive in thy womb, and bring forth a son, and shalt call his name Jesus.

He shall be great and shall be called the Son of the Highest: and the Lord God shall give unto him the throne of his father David:

And he shall reign over the house of Jacob for ever; and of his kingdom there shall be no end.

THE HOLY GHOST shall come upon thee, and the power of the Highest shall overshadow thee; therefore also that holy thing that shall be born of thee shall be called the Son of God.

And Mary said, Behold the handmaid of the Lord; be it unto me according to thy word. And the angel departed from her.

And it came to pass in those days, that there went out a decree from Caesar Augustus, that all the world should be taxed.

And all went to be taxed, every one into his own city.

A ND JOSEPH also went up from Galilee, out of the city of Nazareth, into Judaea, unto the city of David, which is called Bethlehem; (because he was of the house and lineage of David).

To be taxed with Mary, his espoused wife, being great with child.

A ND SO IT was, that while they were there, the days were accomplished that she should be delivered.

And she brought forth her firstborn son, and wrapped him in swaddling clothes, and laid him in a manger: because there was no room for them in the inn.

AND THERE were in the same country shepherds abiding in the field, keeping watch over their flock by night.

And, lo, the angel of the Lord came upon them, and the glory of the Lord shone round about them; and they were sore afraid.

And the angel said unto them, Fear not: for, behold, I bring you good tidings of great joy, which shall be to all people.

For unto you is born this day in the city of David a Saviour, which is Christ the Lord.

And this shall be a sign unto you: Ye shall find the babe wrapped in swaddling clothes, lying in a manger.

And suddenly there was with the angel a multitude of the heavenly host praising God and saying,

Glory to God in the highest, and on earth peace, goodwill toward men.

AND IT CAME to pass, as the angels were gone away from them into heaven, the shepherds said one to another, Let us now go even unto Bethlehem, and see this thing which is come to pass, which the Lord hath made known unto us.

And they came with haste, and found Mary, and Joseph, and the babe lying in a manger.

OW BEHOLD there came wise men from the east to Jerusalem, Saying, Where is he that is born King of the Jews? for we have seen his star in the east, and are come to worship him.

WHEN HEROD the king had heard these things, he was troubled, and all Jerusalem with him,
And when he had gathered all the chief priests and scribes of the people together, he demanded of them where Christ should be born.

And they said unto him, In Bethlehem of Judaea: for thus it is written by the prophet,

And thou Bethlehem, in the land of Juda, art not least among the princes of Juda, for out of thee shall come a Governor, that shall rule my people Israel.

Then Herod, when he had privily called the wise men, inquired of them diligently what time the star appeared.

And he sent them to Bethlehem, and said, Go and search diligently for the young child, and when ye have found him, bring me word again, that I may come and worship him also.

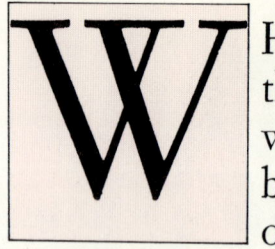WHEN THEY had heard the king, they departed; and, lo, the star, which they saw in the east, went before them, till it came and stood over where the young child was.

When they saw the star, they rejoiced with exceeding great joy.

And when they were come into the house, they saw the young child with Mary, his mother, and fell down, and worshipped him: and when they had opened their treasures, they presented unto him gifts: gold, and frankincense, and myrrh.

AND BEING warned of God in a dream that they should not return to Herod, they departed into their own country another way.

And when they were departed, behold, the angel of the Lord appeareth to Joseph in a dream, saying, Arise and take the young child and his mother, and flee into Egypt, and be thou there until I bring thee word; for Herod will seek the young child to destroy him.

When he arose, he took the young child and his mother by night, and departed into Egypt.

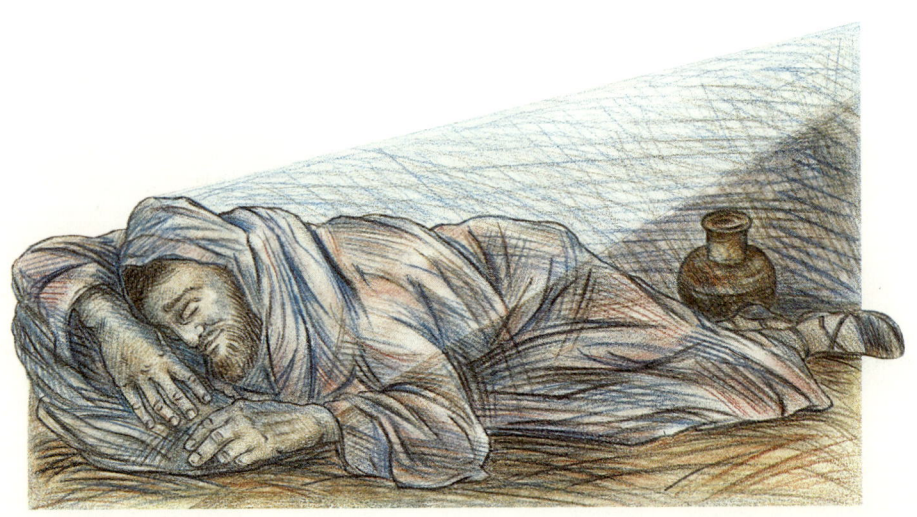

THE PEOPLE that walked in darkness have seen a great light: they that dwell in the land of the shadow of death, upon them hath the light shined.

For unto us a child is born, unto us a son is given; and the government shall be upon his shoulder: and his name shall be called, Wonderful, Counsellor, The mighty God, The everlasting Father, The Prince of Peace.

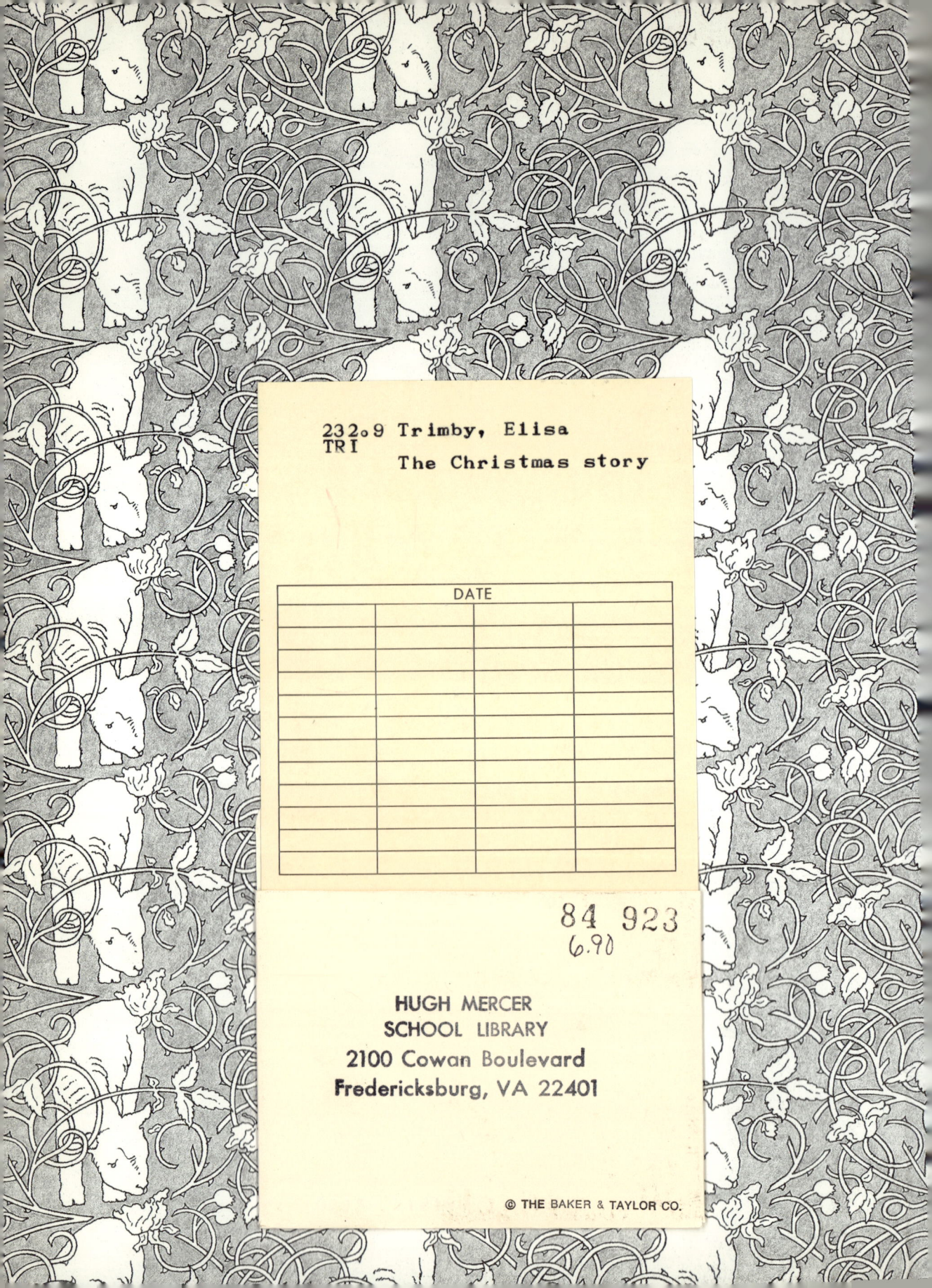

232.9 Trimby, Elisa
TRI   The Christmas story

84 923
6.90

**HUGH MERCER
SCHOOL LIBRARY
2100 Cowan Boulevard
Fredericksburg, VA 22401**

© THE BAKER & TAYLOR CO.